MW01515449

BLACKMAN REDEMPTION
MY MORNING TALKS/PRAYERS WITH GOD

Ah African Pride
Beauty
Life; Paradise

Truth is life and we are life
All comes from God – Good God
Hence all is Black
The black in me and you

Out of the darkness we came into the light
But the light knoweth us not.

We gave the light life
All that is good and true but the light turned against us.
So into the darkness we went again where we cannot be
found.
We became the night; but allowed the light of the moon to
come in to light your way so that you could find home
once again.

We are cherished
Hence life is you and me
Its truth
True love
Truly God given

Life is in the stars; all, hence we are to cherish all. All that
is good and true.

Michelle Jean

Good God it's Saturday morning and I have to ask; what do you truly love and truly like about me?

Yesterday I went to lunch and this White Lady said I was pretty. Thank you for letting someone see your true beauty in me.

I enjoyed lunch at Mandarin but I ate way too much. Good God I over ate and it was if my belly was ready to pop. Hence I learned never over eat again. Never overstuff your belly to beyond its capacity. Hence it does not pay to be greedy.

Good God I was downtown but not fully downtown. Paul said the area we were in was the beginning of downtown.

Good God wow because I saw different faces. And I told him never to bring me back to that area because I thought the people were crazy. Wow Good God because this is the place of the crazies to me.

I don't know but I am so not use to this. Yes I am used to Jamaican crazies – crazy people but I am so not used to Canadian White and Black crazies. I was in a different world and I truly did not like it. Therefore, I so don't want to ever go back there. I thoroughly enjoyed my lunch at

Mandarin. Good God I truly love Chinese Food and I may seem biased but I am truly not.

But Good God; has humanity come this far in life without knowing self; who they are?

No don't answer that because we have hence the world gone crazy – fulfillment time by Smokie Benz and Tony Tuff and World Gone Mad by Ritchie Stephenson featuring Gentleman and Alborosie.

Good God the more I see is the more I truly don't want to be amongst people in society. It's as if we are searching for something and that something we cannot find.

Wi gone Good God; truly gone.

We are not civilized anymore. We have truly become the walking dead. Revelations. Hence man to man is so unjust. Bob Marley.

How can we as humans cling to a society that has failed us all around?

How can we say we are civilized when there is so much evils going on?

We do wrong and look at humanity.

From what I saw yesterday Good God we've truly become lost. Therefore, Revelations was not wrong when it said we are the first begotten of the dead.

We walk like the dead and talk like the dead; hence we've become dead and this is a crying shame.

Dear God it looks as if we've become hopeless. We have no hope at all and this is sad.

Good God is this the reality of man in so called modern and civilized society?

What makes us civilized Good God when there are so many crazies globally?

As humans we cannot see the fakeness of it all. Nor do we know that fakeness kills.

We have fake foods.
Chemically induced foods.
Foods that are genetically modified.

Animals that is chemically induced and genetically selected.

Water that is chemically cleaned; treated.

Polluted air.

Medications that are made from this and that chemical (s).

Humans brainwashed by religion.

Humans living the cosmetic dream.

Fake Skin   Fake Hair   Fake Tan
Fake Breasts   Fake Eyes

Fake Butt   Fake Legs   Fake Lips
Fake Meat   Fake Everything.

This is the life of us as human beings – so called civilized society I guess. Everything is fake including fake vaginas and fake penises. Good God some of these men need to listen to Wally British when it comes to exposing their junk – penis in magazines and social media outlets.

Dear God some a dem a prop up inna magazine and on the internet and don't know what they call size is what some of us use microscopes to see and tweezers to find.

Like I've said before, some women, Caribbean woman wi laugh dem to shame and sey way dat. Dem scaane dem fi dem likkle weenie. Do not pose up what you do not have. Some of you men should stop embarrassing yourselves because the size of your ocean and motion cannot cut it;

hence unnu oman cheat pan unnu. No, for real Good God. I am one to see a nice junk – penis and say wow. But what I've seen lately is nothing to write home to mom – you about. Some men have their penis photo shopped. Some even buy fake props and or strap ons to put on their junk to say they are that big and fat.

Laade truly have mercy because I still equate a man's junk – penis to their shoe size. If you don't have what it takes stop embarrassing yourself. It's gotten to the point where men are having cosmetic surgery to get size; a bigger penis. This is just nasty and insane, Yuk. Hence fake everything.

So yes, the people of this world have and has gone crazy. It's becoming rare to find natural beauty. Everything is so fake I have to wonder how the world – Earth keeps spinning with all the fakeness in her.

Good God we are not natural anymore. We've become chemically dependent, engineered and genetically modified. Everything is massed produced chemically – our food, the diseases of man, cosmetics including man. All this we do for so called perfection. As humans we give up natural beauty for cosmetic tricks and gimmicks. Now look at some that have given up natural beauty for sin. Billions spent globally. And what they call beauty is truly ugly.

We've become chemically dependent. Drugs laced with chemicals we have to take to maintain and sustain our lives if we are sick and want to live. All that we do, we are chemically dependent on drugs and food. Drugs and food that slowly alter our DNA and kills you.

Drugs and food including chemically cleaned water that make us sick and literally drive us crazy – mentally insane; depressed.

All this man did to man. But we, including me wonder why you cannot help us Good God. Why can't you interfere for the better good and not the better evil?

You are Good God but yet you have to sit and wait on time like the rest of us; why?

Why allot 24000 years to evil when you knew evil was going to do all to kill all?

Good God, I too am wondering. Wondering why you cannot stop the madness of so called modern day society and let there be infinite and indefinite peace and tranquility to all.

We are killing self Good God. And the ones we trust are the ones to hurt us; leave us for dead.

Hence I ask again, how do you look at man?

Does it not repent you to see how we are living?

How can you love us so when we are so vile and wicked?

How can you love us so when we destroy everything including you?

Tell me now, is your loving is so because we kill and do everything that is evil in thy sight?

Or is your loving us so the fact that billions are going to die in hell shortly; real soon?

Is this loving us so for the death, true death of us; man – humanity?

Wow Good God because we do not know that this is the society of death. All we do is designed to kill and do nothing to preserve; truly live.

Michelle Jean

Good God I've talked about the physical and world a lot but what about the spiritual world?

Why is your world closed to me? I mean I need you but yet cannot reach you my way.

I need to talk to you but cannot see you.........no I can. You let me see you when you want to. So forget this line of questioning because there is no merit to it. So let's talk about the spiritual realm because this world does affect me and I truly do not know why? I mean there are negative spirits and some do hinder you in the living and I truly do not know why? There is more to the spiritual realm but yet I cannot comprehend why spiritual evil have to hurt man – humans? Yes what I've written before stands but the fight that good gets from evil is beyond me.

Evil destroy everything.

Evil kills but yet humanity cannot see the evils that they have done.

Good God this is so beyond me. Hell we created yes, but why can't we lock away all spiritual evil indefinitely?

I see so much but permanently and indefinitely shutting down spiritual evil – all evil forever ever I cannot do. Why?

Good God we cannot continue to allow spiritual evil to affect us. Yes I know good have nothing to do with evil but Good God are we all evil?

Is the air, water, trees, food of the ground, all animals including the fish of the sea – waters evil as well?

Good God am I evil when it comes to you?

Do not be shocked because you knew I would ask this question eventually. I truly love you unconditionally and more than universally but is my true love true love?

I speak to you and write to you but yet you rarely answer me. So am I writing in vain and in thought when it comes to you?

There are things I need to know, things I need to do but yet you do not permit me to.

There are things I need to know but yet you do not allow me to know.

The true you I cannot see but yet you say you love us so. I don't know Good God because I cannot break down the confines of your walls and rest with you. Maybe it's not time yet. But then you said you keep building and I keep breaking down. And like I said, you are God – Good God and Allelujah, how can I break down what you have built?

I've talked to you about foundations and if you don't build good and true; impenetrable foundations that can never be broken, how can we be true to you?

Will we not come and build faulty foundations also?

If God – Good God and Allelujah is faulty, we will be faulty also.

If you cannot build good and everlasting foundations of goodness and truth; clean and positive energy, how are you expecting us to?

If we were raised in lies, will we not grow up to tell lies?

Will we not become liars?

If you say you love us so, how can we then love you true? And take me out of the mix because I was born with truth and was taught true love not just by you but by my true and beautiful mother in her own way.

Yes I know the scope and greatness of loving so but what about the scope and greatness of loving true? What about the scope and greatness of staying true and doing all that is good and true?

Ah Good God, you are my true Breath of Life hence I cannot love you so, I must love you true.

Michelle Jean

Ah man I'm getting side tracked because I so want to get into the spiritual world but you won't let me Good God.

Maybe this is not the time and place for it.

Oh Good God I want and need a wedding ring.

Do you think 2015 you will permit me to get married?

Yes I know my marriage to you which is our bond of truth.

Your marriage to us is different. It's not how nor is it like how humans marry each other.

When you marry us it's like saying you are my child and you are a part of my good, true and clean world. We become your messengers and teachers of goodness and truth, peace and true love, cleanliness. Good God you are like our adopted parents if we do not have your true name. Yes explaining our relationship to others when it comes to you is different because we are under your banner and name. But for those that have your true name we are your true descendants; children by marriage and birth hence the Jews – Jew. You are our morning dew, meaning you are our waters of life hence we come from your realm with you embedded in our true DNA.

Good God, I know my rights with you but can you ordain the right someone for me so that in 2015 me and that good clean, positive, truly loving someone that you ordain for me can get married?

I know I know I'm asking a lot but I truly need this now.

Remember when I was in the hospital last month and how lonely I felt. Yes I had my son and Brianna there with me but yet I felt lonely.

You weren't there to hold my hand and say everything is going to be okay.

I had no husband or mate rushing to my side to stay with me and give me moral support.

I had no friends to come by and lend moral support.

You didn't even send an angel or two. Yes I had my son and Briana like I said, but I needed you to be there for me. I need someone because in life it's not good for anyone to be lonely. And I truly can't handle the loneliness anymore.

Good life isn't about oneness or loneliness, it's about togetherness; truth. It's like you need me but yet you are pulling away from me and this does not make any sense to me. If you say you love us so, then why continue to run and or pull away from us?

We all need life Good God. So if you are getting truth, why do I feel as if you are running from this truth; you don't want it? I don't know with you anymore. But the one thing I do know is that I need the trees.

I need the waters of this world.

I need Mother Earth and all of her beauty.

I need you but I truly do not need your loneliness.

To be honest with you Good God, in my world loneliness is depression; a sin hence no one should be lonely in life. I know at times many of us say they don't need anyone and to me this is a lie. We are lying to self. We all need someone Good God even if that someone is you.

I truly need to get out more but where I need to go is far far away.

I need to walk in the sun.

Sleep under the moonlight.

Walk on a sandy beach; my own.

I need to talk with you but truly not here. Not here in the land I am living in. Too cold and I truly need to get away from here; the cold.

Ah Good God loneliness sucks.

Loneliness deprives you of life.

Loneliness makes you feel dead – unwanted.
Yes loneliness sucks to high hell. So why would you want and need this, loneliness for me or anyone Good God?

Yes I truly love solitude but solitude isn't lonely I guess.

I'm a true nature lover. Hence I need to live in nature with nature and you.

I need the trees of life hence I must be surrounded by trees. Green trees; all the green trees of nature that you truly gave me.

I need to dance
Be happy

I need to laugh

I need to grow strong, so why do you keep me lonely?

Why allow me to die of loneliness?

And no civilized society is truly not for me because I find nothing civilized in modern day societies.

Yes modern civilization of death. I live for life, all that is good and true Good God and you need to do the same.

Michelle Jean

You know Good God, forgiveness goes both ways but yet I find myself stupid – living a stupid life.

I have children that have no ambition for self.

Have no ambition to excel in school – life.

Good God, today I am asking you this in the physical and spiritual to let me find a good place and move far away from my children.

Good God and Allelujah, just as how you left man in the physical and spiritual for the better good of you, please let me do so with my children.

Not through death but just by me finding a good, positive, clean and true place in the physical and spiritual for me and you. I truly cannot take the life I am living nor can I take and live with ambitionless children anymore. I truly need to go and go now where they can't find me.

As a parent you try your best to give your children a better future but they are the ones to not want it. Then later in life they turn trouble to you.

Good God there is good children out there that need an education, but can't get it.

There are good children out there that need medical care, but can't get it.

There are good children out there that need food, but parents can't afford to give them food.

There are good children out there that need a home – roof over their heads, but can't get it and in goodness and in truth, I need to help these good people.

I need them to have hope – a better and good future; tomorrow with you. My children are truly not deserving of my goodness except for one. I will truly help him but the others I truly do not care to help because of cleanliness and lack of ambition. Good God you are my earthly mother and father in the spiritual and in the physical. I made you this because you made me your child in both realms. And besides I have your beautiful and gorgeous name. Thus saith the Lord thy God meaning it is so. And yes I am proud to have your name.

You know my true love of you hence I must do good and true by you in the physical and spiritual realm. And because of this, I truly have to walk away from the unclean environment that I am living in in both realms; world.

I cannot live clean in an unclean environment and surroundings; world.

I cannot live with children that cause me pain and sufferings; embarrassment in the physical and spiritual world.

I cannot live with children that cannot see and want a better tomorrow for self in the physical and spiritual realm.

I cannot live with children that refuse to live a clean and positive life. I need my physical and spiritual world to be pure and clean; void of all sin and sins infinitely and indefinitely forever ever. But I cannot have this living with sinful and wicked children, children that don't listen to good council. Children that cannot see the greater good of what I am trying to do for them. I know spiritual and physical evils and in all that I've tried to do, I've tried to shield them from these evils with the good that I try to do. Evil is evil Good God, so why should I let my children go into the fire if I can prevent it? I refuse death and they should too. But I cannot force my children to see because they have their own minds. Some don't want to know but it's their decision, the decision that they made. They are the ones to feel it real soon and like I've told you, I will not be there for them because they refuse to listen. Just as how Eve disobeyed you and locked herself out of your abode indefinitely forever ever, I will do the same to my own. I cannot continually talk to them for their own good and they are not listening. At some point in time you have to walk away and like you, this is what I need to do as of 2015 January 1. This is for our better good Good God hence I will not budge from this date. Even if I have to live in the streets I will do it because I am truly tired. My health is not improving and I have to think of me and truly being with you in goodness and in truth indefinitely. Not through the death of my flesh but through true peace and harmony, goodness and cleanliness; positivity.

Good God you see the disrespect I get from my children. I know I had a tiff with my mother when I was younger hence I too disrespected her. I too did not listen when she tried to save me. So yes this is my punishment for not listening to her. I am facing it hence Mother, Rosalind Rosetta Morgan truly forgive me for all the wrongs I've done to you. I know now that you were trying to protect me but I could not listen nor did I listen. Father God, truly thank you for my wonderful and beautiful mother. She did try but as kids, children sometimes we don't understand nor comprehend. Hence I tell my children all that I see that pertains to them. Maybe I need to do a better job with them but what can you do when you get please don't talk to me sometimes? Or I am a big man I can do what I want or make my own decisions. You are going the wrong way listen to good council when it comes to paying your bills and the company you choose.

Good God, I truly don't know sometimes. Sometimes I feel like a failure when it comes to them. Good God like you, a good and true parent that truly loves their children do not want to see them hurt. So we do all to protect them from the evils out there. As a good parent you try your best so that your children will have a better and good tomorrow positively. I need this for them and my, well our future generations that come from our DNA; family. Yes this includes the seeds you've given me because these people are our true family too.

We're all physical and spiritual beings Good God and I cannot take the nonsense of sin and evil anymore.

I did not come into this world to live a life of sin spiritually and physically. I came in this world to live a good and clean life, a life void of all sin and evil.

Like I said, I can't take it anymore hence I ask you for Goodness and Truth, Honesty and Cleanliness, Positivity and all that is true and just in my life. Not just physically but spiritually indefinitely.

A life of sin is not worth it hence I ask forgiveness for all my sins in the physical and spiritual world infinitely and indefinitely without end forever ever.

Good God, I truly cannot continue to live this way. I cannot continue to live amongst sinful children that have no ambition for self and you; their surroundings. Old people sey, ambition goes a far and they are infinitely and indefinitely correct.

When you have ambition you excel. You want and need better for self; all that is around you and all that surrounds you.

When you are around ambitionless people you cannot excel. Hence negative energy makes you sick; kills you in the end.

Yes sometimes I question my purpose in life. I also question you but hey I am learning no matter my yoyo feelings when it comes to truth and you. Yes sometimes I slip in the truth department but I come to you hence I am truly sorry for all the lies I've told in my life. I too have faults and I recognize them hence I have to do better in the total and infinite truth department. Meaning I have to do better when it comes to sliding with my kids. There are no half truths just full and pure truths. It's October 28th 2014 and my son wanted to use my USB but I did not want to let him use it. I had No Weapons by Fred Hammond going and I am writing this book. Well putting what I've written on paper on my USB stick. He asked me if I would lose my data and I told him yes. I gave him the USB stick knowing full well that I would not lose my written stuff but I would lose my media player. Meaning the song would stop playing. Yes I can lose my data if he doesn't bring my stick back for me to save it. I know I can save my data on my desktop or use another USB, but it's the fact that I did not want him to use my USB. Yes I am picky when it comes to my things. And no I am not being mean because my son is capable of buying his own USB and putting his music on it. My USB's are for my books and my music but my kids believe its shareware. And they do share hence I have shared USB's.

Like I said, I need honesty and cleanliness and I have to have this in the physical and spiritual world because I am both physical and spiritual. Hence the mate you send me must be this way as well. The mate you send me must be clean and honest, good and positive; honest and true in both worlds; the physical and spiritual. Further, any grandchildren of mine and future generations must be infinitely and indefinitely forever ever without end, good and true, positive and clean, honest and just, pure and good, righteous and honest in all that they do. They must be upright and righteous beyond measure. No sin must they do infinitely and indefinitely forever ever without end. They must be totally pure and just, righteous, good and clean, honest and kind indefinitely. Absolutely no lies must come from their lips or them. Their children must come and walk in the same manner of goodness and truth infinitely and indefinitely without end. They too must be just, honest, kind and clean, good and pure indefinitely forever ever without end for more than infinite and indefinite lifetimes and generations. Good God their children must be the same; good and clean, just. The goodness and cleanliness; purity of soul and spirit (physical and spiritual) that I ask of you in this prayer is binding. It is our marriage of truth for more than indefinite lifetimes and generations forever ever without end. Everyone must be good and true to you; truth. All when they don't ask of this you Good God and Allelujah you must give them good and true children that are pure and righteous, good and clean, positive and just in all that they do. No sin must they do. No lies must they tell. They must be void of all sin and evil indefinitely without end. Like I've said, I did not know this so now I know and I am exercising my right of truth and true love to you. This goodness I also ask in truth for the seeds you've given me and their children and children's children. **Good God this must be our good and true NEW WORLD ORDER. Good God, GOOD MUST MARRY GOOD FROM NOW ON. WE CAN NO LONGER WED AND OR MARRY EVIL. THIS IS I NEED BECAUSE I TRULY NEED YOU AND TRULY LOVE YOU WITHOUT END.**

If only you trusted me like I trusted you Good God.

If only you could need me as I need you.

If only you could feel what I feel in the womb. Yes the tears come but you cannot feel what I feel. You cannot feel that truth and true love inside of me. Hence it grieves me to know that you have people that truly love you, truly need you but yet you can't let them find you and be at rest, true rest and peace with you. Hence see my tears of truth

Good God and help me to make this truth a reality for all Lyon and Lyons including my true family and the seed and seeds you've given me. I need to hold on Good God. I need to forever ever hold on to our goodness. I need to help Good God, so rise me up to help your people as well as build you your good and true home. Maybe this home can be a log cabin mansion in the woods by the rivers of your water. But please let me build you a good home made out of true love and goodness; pure and unconditional truth.

Good God, why can't we be upright and just, honest and clean, pure, positive and good infinitely and indefinitely forever ever without end?

No evil must we walk in indefinitely. And Good God this is not just a physical asking but a spiritual asking also. This asking must last infinitely and indefinitely from generation unto generation forever ever without end universally in the spiritual realm.

All the goodness and truth that I miss please add them to my asking of goodness and truth Good God in truth and honesty positively.

Michelle Jean

You know sometimes I want to lose you Good God hence 2015 January 1 is the date I gave you for me to leave you. Well to step aside and let you and death handle your business.

I cannot take the dirty environment I am living in and you are doing nothing to truly save me.

My children are older now and of age. It's time for me to go and make a new start. A new start based on pure cleanliness, truth, true love; the true you.

I can no longer live a dirty life nor can I fight – quarrel with my children for their better good.

I truly can't anymore. I truly have to go and find me; my new world.

I cannot live amongst filth and hate anymore.

I cannot, truly cannot live with the disrespect anymore. I have to go and truly make myself pure and true; truly clean. Where I am at, I am not clean. I have to truly do for me hence truly doing for you.

My time which is our time has come and we have to be totally clean in both worlds. We cannot be clean half way, we must be clean full way. We need this Good God. So truly help me for the better physically and spiritually in goodness and in truth; the better good of me and you – humanity.

Good God I want and need to give positively but how can I give good and true positively when I am being hindered spiritually and physically by you? If you don't want to share me just say so, but truly stop hindering me because I am not hindering you. Giving good and positive; clean and true is my right because I am looking to you for all that is good and true. I am looking to you for infinite and indefinite joy and happiness infinitely and indefinitely forever ever without end.

Michelle Jean

Good God and Allelujah, I need my world and universes to be clean spiritually and physically. So why keep me in an environment that I am truly not happy in?

Why keep me in a place that is causing me true pain?

I am looking for you to help me out of my environment indefinitely so I may never ever return to an environment of hardship and pain ever again. So why are you not truly helping me?

Everywhere I turn there are obstacles in my way. When will it end Good God? When will it end?

Tell me something. How can you be there for me if I am surrounded by sin as well as living in a dirty environment – place?

I cannot rise. All I am doing is falling and I am tired of falling.

I am tired of being stuck between heaven and hell. Yes it's one of my novels; Between Heaven and Hell. But I am tired of being stuck between heaven and hell. I need to break the physical and spiritual spell that impedes and or hinder me. I need to get hold of my spiritual and physical life and make them truly clean – pure. This I cannot do by myself. I truly need your good and positive help. I am not getting any younger in physical and spiritual age. So truly help me and lets come together in a positive, good, true and clean way.

Good God if my physical world is untidy then my spiritual world will be untidy also. I live like the poor and as the poor in the physical. So because of this I will live like the poor and as the poor in the spiritual also. And I am so not about that anymore because you did not make poor, man did.

Good God, I do not need the mindset of humans. I need the mindset of the good and true; you, the truly civilized and educated; knowledgeable in the physical and spiritual realm. You know me when it comes to education and truth. So please stop the physical and spiritual hindering on my part. My life in the spiritual and physical is not a game. So truly do all that is good, honest, pure, clean, positive and true to help me in both worlds.

Michelle Jean

Good God why is it that every place I've looked at for us to live in you've rejected?

Why is it every place I've looked for help in promoting our books I cannot use?

It's as if the physical and spiritual world is against the avenues I go in and I truly don't know why.

I found the right home in Calgary, Alberta but you rejected it. So you know what, I am going to leave well enough alone. I can't please you because you are too hard to please. Yes there are beautiful places to live but I refuse to live in the United States of America. Not interested in that land. Yes there are beautiful places in the Miami, Florida, Georgia and Arizona but I refuse these places. They are not me and I know I will not be happy there. Good God in truth, I truly have no desire to live and or visit that land. And no I refuse to entertain the thought of building your mega mansion there. I truly love you too much to do so.

Land too damned wicked and dirty. They are deaths land because when death look at sin, the United States of America is what death sees. So why the hell would I entertain or even build you your mega mansion in filth – filthy land?

Right now I have to force myself to go there in 2015 and I truly don't want to do this but I have no other choice. You refuse to make a true way for me to go somewhere else that I can truly afford.

I need an escape and your people (our people) need to escape that land and soon. Truth does not mean death Good God come on now. You need some place clean and so far you've rejected my choosing. I truly don't know what else to do. So, when you are truly ready for your home of goodness and truth and cleanliness, truly let me know.

Michelle Jean
October 25, 2014

You know something Good God we are truly picky.

Yes you know my good intention of thee as well as the desired place I have in mind for thee. So in your going out and coming in, review my intentions of goodness and truth and lead me clearly and securely, peacefully and positively to the right place to build your mega mansion.

Good God, I do not want to pick wrong or buy wrong.

Good God this is for you; us and I don't want to choose wrong. So truly help me to be right all the time unconditionally forever ever in goodness and in truth without end.

You mean too much to me hence I don't want to hurt you or displease you in anyway.

So please truly listen to me. I need you to hear me and lift me up in your good and true, clean and honest blessings and prosperity. It's hard Good God when you have to pray around dirty people and things. This morning I am listening to I NEED THEE by Tamela Mann.

Good God like she said, "I can't fix it, I've tried everything else. Lord I come to...."

Good God I too have tried and failed. I can't do it all by myself. I need you to truly help me to fix all that is broken in my life and your people's lives. The stage of desperation comes. Many will be lost and if we do not have you now, we will never have you.

This harvest will be brutal because many lands will be lost due to destruction. Hence I tell you to gather your people so that we can ride out the storm and storms that are coming our way with you.

We can't run no more Good God and you cannot continue to run from us. It's time to stand and take hold of your good and true people not the fake ones.

Yes I know we are living in a dirty planet. But truly do not let my prayers be dirty or become dirty because I am living in an unclean place and environment; world.

Good God I know we caused this on self because we listened to the voices of deceit – evil.

We listened to religion and the lies and deceit of religion.

We listened to generational lies that spew hate and hatred for others.

We listened to biblical lies and false accounts of the truth.

We listened to mans so called societal truths; conditioning and lies.

But with all that said Good God, we truly need you in this day and time. It is going to get brutal real soon for man and without you, we are going to die. Earth must comply with the truth of life and let wicked and evil people including wicked and evil spirits go. She can no longer house them nor can she continue to give them a home.

Good God I am trying to be clean you know this. So truly hear me. Please make a way for us to communicate clearly and cleanly. Allelujah, this is all I have. I have nothing to offer you a part from my truth and unconditional love. So please help me to make me and my prayers clean and true to you always and forever ever.

Michelle Jean

Wow this morning Lord because I need you right now. I need to know that we are safe with each other forever ever without end. Well at least you are with me.

Good God it is not my intention to give you anything dirty. Not even dirty prayers, but how can I make my prayers fully clean unto you living amongst sin? How can I Good God? How can I?

All that I've chosen for you is wrong Good God. Why?

Why are you displeased with my choices?

Wow because the fairness of life is gone from man and I feel as if it's gone from me and you also. Maybe I want and need; yearn too much for us Good God and Allelujah.

You are my true love but I can't take the lies; closed doors and windows of you when it comes to me and you anymore.

2014 is coming to an end – close but yet I am not further ahead than when I started. My life is too hard and painful when it comes to you. The tears are there but yet you can't see me; help me.

It's as if I am stuck in the same position with you. As if I have no real growth and growth potential with you and this is wrong an all angles.

You can't help me nor can you direct me on the right path. So why am I holding on to you if you cannot direct me properly?

You're suppose to be our father, the one we can run to for advice but the advice is not forthcoming from you. All is delayed; stuck.

It's as if we are a broken truck in my book. I've been stuck at start for years and each step I take to leave the start position and continue on our journey I am stuck. I can't go. Your engine refuse to start and or turn over for the betterment of us, our land and family; people.

Good God are your batteries dead?

Do you need a jump start to get you going?

Good God you need to do better in the betterment and prosperity department. You need your mega mansion and you've shown me the house you need, but I cannot get to that land if you don't help me properly.

I can't seek all the time Good God come on now.

I am tired, truly tired of writing and you are not hearing me; nor are you helping me.

I cannot live in vain with you anymore. I need total truth and trust.

I need cleanliness, positive energy and goodness unconditionally in all that I do not just for you but for myself; others.

Good God why should there be this distance between us?

Did evil not fail? So why do you continue to hurt me in this way?

I cannot continue to listen to you and you are not listening to me. One sided relationships fail. They do not work Good God. So why are you failing me?

Why are you the one sided one in our good and true relationship?

Why do you set me up for failure?

Michelle Jean

I need to run away from it all Good God. I even need to run away from you temporarily.

Now I am scheduled to go into a land that I truly don't want or need to go in.

Good God can't we find a better way because I truly don't want to go to LA. You know this but I guess I have to go.

Yes I am hurt and it pains me that I can't go someplace else but this is the story of my life; always wanting and needing when it comes to you. You make me feel like a damned failure because I put all my trust in you but yet you cannot trust me; put all your trust in me.

I am hurt Good God. Can't you see this? I yearn and need truth unconditionally from you but you can't give this to me.

I truly don't want to go to LA hence I am coming to you with my unconditional truth and you are ignoring me. Yes I know your distance in time and you cannot speed up time to please and accommodate me, but why not? Yes I know this is a spoilt child speaking, but why can't you fix the space time continuum and or help me fix all that is wrong in my life including the distance between me and you; space and time?

Ah Allelujah if all was perfect and true in all that we do I would not have to nag you so. And knowing me I would probably keep you locked away all to myself. Not, got to share you with our true loves ones and lovey. I'm not the only one that truly loves you but it feels like it to me.

Allelujah, do you cry for me like I cry for you? Do you desire and yearn for perfect and unconditional peace and cleanliness like I do?

All these things I desire and yearn for. Yes I desire and yearn for more but unfortunately you cannot accept me as I am and this is sad. I accept you for you just as you are but you can't accept me. I feel as if I am not the one you need, hence I am stepping aside as of 2015 January 1. So you take care and be true to you because you cannot be fully true to me hence the loving us so.

Michelle Jean

As humans we refuse to know and know the truth.

We refuse to lean that separation from all that is wicked and evil is the best and or right thing to do for man; humanity including you Good God.

We refuse to know and learn that when you Good God and Allelujah have deemed a nation and land unclean, we cannot go into that land ever. No one can go back in that land if they are from there. You cannot vacation in that land either.

We as Black People refuse to learn this hence we praise and worship death like fools. I cannot be like them hence I refuse and condemn all facets of religion whether physical or spiritual.

I refuse to let religion dirty me anymore because life cannot be a religion, it can only be life; the truth infinitely and indefinitely forever ever without end.

Good Life is based on the truth; true love hence good life was created in truth; true love.

In all that we do Good God you do not stop us from accumulating wealth and enjoying a good life. The problem and issue comes in when we become untrue and dirty in our day to day dealings; living. We cannot pray to man and death and think we are going to be okay because we are not.

Our life isn't the life of a man. Our life is spirit not man – flesh and we are to live our life good and clean. Like I've said time and time again, the flesh is just a prison for the spirit.

Yes you can consider the flesh as the home or house of the spirit, hence we must clean our spirit by eating clean food and meat not unclean things. Water must be clean hence it is advisable to boil your tap water and cool it (the boiled water) before drinking it.

The taste is truly different. Hence the taste of true rain water; clean and crisp – refreshing. Hence in all that Allelujah and Good God deals in is good and true; clean.

Michelle Jean
October 25, 2014

"OUT OF MANY ONE PEOPLE," but we are not all your people Good God.

We do not all follow you. Nor are we united with you.

We do not all listen to you. So how could we be one people when different races of different flags; religion and creed worship other gods?

How could we be one people when we kill and destroy not just self and the environment – Mother Earth but you?

How could we be one people when we are not all clean?

Good God, you told me you remembered us. So truly remember and truly save your good and true own; children and people.

No matter how we are forsaken and left for dead, you are right there with us.

No matter the hatred you have not forgotten us even when we feel forsaken by you. Just yesterday I dreamt this little dark boy. He was dark (a black child) and I thought he was you. I believe he said he needed me but do not fully quote me; but it was lovely. I remember trying to hold on to that dream in the living and I rest my head on his shoulder as if comforting self. It feels truly good and wonderful to be truly needed Good God. Do you know how blessed you are Good God?

Do you? You have truth and true love and the greatest gift that you could have given me was that. To feel need and wanted by a child; you. I have you and no matter my complaints to you and you know I will never stop nagging you in this way but truly, truly, truly thank you for needing me. Thank you for not forgetting us – your people. It is your people that must do right and true by you right now.

You've given me life and hope because you need me.

You've given me a future that is good and true not just in your world but in our world. I needed to hear that. I needed your truth. So thank you for good and true life from the womb; my true heart.

Michelle Jean
October 29, 2014

I am not so alone now Good God and Allelujah. Truly thank you.

You know my feel as the going to LA but if this is the place you want me to be then I will not deny you your right to talk to your people. If it be thy will let me truly help you to prepare your people and lead them out of the belly of the beast.

Remember Marcus Mosiah Garvey tried and the people of America did not listen to him nor did they accept him. Hence they failed you and him and now the cost to them they cannot repay nor will they ever repay.

Good God, this is it, the final journey for your people in the land of sin and evil. Life – the flags of life and triangle of life has and have been taken from them and handed back to you. Hence let thy will be done in goodness and in truth. Amen

"OUT OF MANY ONE PEOPLE," hence you have but one people. One true child – nation that truly loves you. You have to gather your people because the gathering comes for them whilst the harvest comes to destroy and take the devils own; all who are wicked and evil.

LIFE AND DEATH IS A CHOICE BUT BILLIONS CHOSE DEATH OVER LIFE.
Good God I know for a fact beyond any doubts you did not lock anyone out of your abode. We as

humans locked ourselves out with our sins and lies.

We are the ones to slam the door shut in your face and this is truly sad.

Like I've said, if you are wicked death does not have to take you. Death can take a family member or even a close friend. This I've come to know. As humans we do not look at our sins and despite death, death is trying to tell humanity, do not sin and come to hell with me because I will let your spirit pay.

We know what evil can do thus we know what death can do.

There are generational sins and they do pass down from family member to family member because sin is engrained in their DNA. Evil cannot overcome evil, evil can only kill evil. Yes good people get caught in the crossfire and this is sad. But as good people we too have to take a look at self. We too have done wrongs hence try to clear up your wrongs by changing the linen of dirty self; wash your body and spirit clean. This can be done but it is hard but yet easy. For me I know what sin and evil is all about. Hence I do not watch the news nor do I follow the news. If someone or my kids do not say mom you know so and so, he got shot and died I will not know.

Death is not my concern hence when death is taking his and her own I am safely tucked away in the arms of God – Good God and Allelujah.

Human life is ending and it will end on a massive scale shortly but this is not my concern because we all knew that his day would come. The time to die we did not know. The hour we do not know. Now you know but the exact time before 2032 I cannot tell you. You have the time frame of death now; use your time left on earth wisely and save self; your own.

Father God, Allelujah and All, you have all my petitions before you and it's time to do right by me and your people. It's time to let death go far far away from your true people. We can no longer live and dine amongst death's people. We must live and dine with you in the land and lands you've prepared for us with your people.

Humanity has the truth pertaining to life and death, but they need the full truth pertaining to you and your cleanliness; living.

You are God alone Allelujah hence you are our Breath of Life.

You are our life source; truth and truths.
You are our waters of life.

I know of the man of old that separated the lands and I am asking you to let him do the same in this day and time. I need your true people to be protected from the storm. Hence truly commission him to complete the final separation not just in land and lands but in us humans as well. Good people must be separated from evil people Good God. And as the North separated from the South, truly let life and your people of the South reign supreme forever more with you without end in goodness and in truth. Good God let us provide for them in truth and true love. Let's give our people and lands hope; a better, brighter and positive tomorrow indefinitely forever ever without end. We must unite firmly in an impenetrable way.

We need you Good God so truly let earth bond with us in marriage; union in a good and true way. Earth is our earthly mother and I am truly proud of her. She keeps us safe from the storms of evil but evil and wicked people have no good will for her. Hence I say we must forgive earth for maintaining and sustaining evil; wicked and evil people including spirits.

Good God as I look to you for all that is good and true. Remember all that is good and true. Evil is not for me and you truly know this. Hence remember not evil in all the good that you do.

Yes I know it had to be this way. You gave us a choice and the latter of us chose evil over good.

Now death comes in time to take all that is wicked and evil.

Goodness and truth be with you always Good God. Goodness and truth be with you always.

We are your people and we truly need to come home.

We need to reach you because this is the final steps of man – humanity.

Earth needs to recover from the ills of man. But with wickedness and evil; wicked and evil men and women including spirits, it is impossible for her to do so.

Truly look to earth and let her abide with you in truth Good God. We can no longer allow humans to kill and destroy because Satan lost. His people lost because one did truly love you and did all that is good for you. Find hope in her and let her do your good will in these the final seconds; years of man in physical terms, the physical and spiritual realm.

Michelle Jean
October 29, 2014

ONWARDS I GO

Good God I cannot fully remember the dream but it has to do with rich – Hollywood White Jews.

Good God, I cannot concern myself with them because the truth must be known and whether we accept it not, it's up to us. Like I've said, these are the final seconds of man in spiritual years and it's up to us to use these final seconds and or earthly years to save self and family.

There is but one door to you Good God and that way is truth; our truth and cleanliness. From you are true you are clean. I cannot make anyone clean nor can you Good God. Good Life was given to man but as man, we do all to destroy good life; the truth and I cannot live like this. I need the truth, true truth in my life each and every day. I've seen hell and the fire that burns and kill the spirit. Hence I have to do all that is good and true to life and in life. Right now the people of earth are living in a mess and it is this mess that's taking us to hell.

We all want but instead of doing good and clean, we do greedily; false. You Allelujah did not create hell. We as humans did with our sins. We cannot blame you for our ills; death Good God and Allelujah. We can only blame self. We caused this final destruction on self. Yes billions are going to die because in all we do, we did not think of the wages, pay of our sins.

We did not think that death is time (6666) not 666 but 24 000 years. The time for death to come and destroy all that is living and dead depending on our sins; evils. So 666 and or 6666 is the time to die. Good cannot be destroyed because good does nothing wrong. Nor does 666 and or 6666 pertain to good. It pertains to evil – the death of wicked and evil people on a massive scale.

Man does wrong. We do wrong daily hence we destroy life; the truth daily.

Michelle Jean

In all I do Good God, I do in goodness and truth of you. But it seems you are the one failing me.

But why Good God?

Lately I've been dreaming about dry and or dried trees.

Just this morning I dreamt about this white woman and her baby. But I could not see her face nor the baby's face. I was inside this house with glass window panes and she was outside. Suffice it to say, I did not let her in. With her outside was this fat dry limb of a tree. Yes I know what his dream means hence it came through with my sister calling me.

Good God I am a recluse. I shut people out including family. Hence my sister called me stubborn. Certain things I do I will not budge or move on and it's going to stay this way.

Yes I am extremely unsociable and don't you dare say ya think. Don't like crowds unless it's on my terms. You know how crowds scare me. I am not a crowd person and will forever be this way. Our people are so different hence I truly love them. Although they are spiritually given, I will receive them in goodness and in truth in the living so long as they are good and true people;

clean. Good people helping good people all the way I say.

So forgive me if I am unsociable or an introvert. Hey this is me. But Good God your people, our people and family cannot be boring like me. They must be fun and outgoing.

Good God my fun is doing, so please do not fail me but let me truly do all in goodness for you my way. Yes our way.

Michelle Jean
October 26, 2014

We truly need to sit and talk Good God.

You have to stop failing me.

You have to stop being as stubborn as me when it comes to me.

Wow. Two stubborn people.
I'm stubborn.
You're stubborn.

Wow. Tell me how are we going to make it in life with our stubbornness?

Ah well got to leave things alone.

Michelle Jean
October 26, 2014

Good God is there a right way to get to you in life; the physical?

Is there a right way when it comes to all with you? Yes I know these are stupid questions but if we do not have a true way with you, how can we know if we are right?

Good God how many others have you asked to write a book?

How many others have failed you in their writings? I have to ask Good God because at times I feel like a failure, feel that I've failed you. But I feel as if you too have failed me.

Good God, why can't it be one book of everlasting truth and goodness we read and learn from?

Good God this book should not include sins book because this is the book of truth; true life. Yes I know life is in stages and you have to give the truth in stages. But why can't there be that one ultimate good and true book that governs all?

I don't know Good God because I still have many questions. Yes I want to run away but will my life be any different? I truly need to do me Good God. I truly need to be with the trees – nature. I have to have my flowing springs with clean beautiful waters that I can drink and bathe in. I need you there too Good God but yet I feel and think you are failing me; have failed me.

Michelle Jean
October 26, 2014

Why can't it be real between me and you Good God? Why do you make me pray in vain to you?

Why do you let me down in life?

I crave and yearn true nature but you keep true nature from me.

I crave and yearn true life but yet you keep me from true life.

Good God what is it with me that you don't truly love me.

Why do you hinder me?

I need the countryside.

I need to kiss a tree, my beautiful trees. Well ours. But they are mine because all your goodness in mine. Well I claim all your goodness just to be greedy when it comes to you. Smile.

Love you lots. Yes I'm batting the eyes and kicking my feet like an innocent child. Ah Good God you are true to me even though I pray this way.

Yes Good God I can go to the United States for a vacation. But I truly, infinitely and indefinitely truly do not want to vacation there. Please I beg of you, truly don't let me vacation there. Please Good God I beg of you with all that is good and true in

Mother Earth and in the spiritual realm and universe not to make me vacation in the valley of sin; the dead. Please do not hurt me like this Good God but truly help me to go someplace else.

Cuba but definitely not the Dominican Republic or Haiti. Keep me the hell out of Haiti and the Dominican; Dominican Republic.

Samoa
Costa Rica
Spain
Africa
Russia
Antarctica – the Southern Seas
France
Scotland
Iceland
New Zealand
The Yukon

Anywhere, no not anywhere but definitely not the valleys of sin. And no, not Bora Bora. Somehow this place is not for me.

Fiji no.
Hawaii no.

China yes.

Korea no, but my daughter wants to go there. Well South Korea and not North Korea. But Korea I don't think is for me. Too vain when it comes to beauty – cosmetic beauty. Beauty is bought and sold there. So no, I truly don't want to go there. The hearts and minds of the people are not clean but vain; deadly and based on pure and utter vanity.

I need to be clean. Please do not let me soil the linen of self by allowing me to go into lands I truly do not want or need to go in. But if it is thy will for me to go into the valley of death; sin; the United States of America to take your people out and or learn, ***then I will do so under your protection and out of good and true will of you and not me. My true will is not to go there but I am also abiding by you Good God.*** And if you desire me to go into this land I will go. ***Not for me like I said, but for you and only you.*** I will not disobey you if you want me to go to these lands. ***But in truth I truly have no good and true desire to go into the United States of America, Haiti and the Dominican Republic.***

Hey Good God there is Brazil and Venezuela but indefinitely not Trinidad; the three dads. Father, Son and Holy Ghost. Yes the three daughters of Eve in physical and land terms – biblical history.

Michelle Jean
October 25 and 29, 2014

Good God a vacation in the Southern Lands and Seas would do me just fine right now. But how do I get there without funds and a place to say?

Good God and Allelujah can you start looking for the right avenue for me to take in all of this vacation wise.

Good God I truly need to go but LA is not on my true to go to list. I have to now force myself to go because this is the only avenue that is open unto me. Why do I have to force myself to go? With myself forcing me to go to LA, I'm I not forcing you to go also. We both know that the United States of America is the valley of death hence Psalms 23. I do not fear evil because evil can only be evil. I cannot fear evil because you are with me. You are my rod and my staff and you are most definitely my comforter in all that I do that is good and true for you and me. Yes some may say this is cocky but you know what Good God, so be it because I truly don't care if anyone say I am cocky. If they had you and know you like I have you and know you then they too would be cocky.

They too would hold their head up in pride; flick their finger with a huge smile on their face whilst strutting down the street saying, I have God – Good God and Allelujah and you don't. Trust me Good God if some could hire a plane and write in the skies saying. My name is Frank Rossi and I have Good God and you don't they would. I would hence these books are our pride and joy, truths.

Good God it's fun to brag about you and if I could brag on wicked and evil people about you, I would but you would not permit me. But it would be fun though. They would know that I have someone that they truly cannot have no matter what they do.

Good God, come on, I would run an ad in the globally newspapers bragging about you. Man if only I could I would. But I can't because you would hold me for sin. Yes I would be knocking a man or woman down when they are down. But Good God why not, they do it to us. They wallow in sin and show us their wicked and sinful deeds. And don't you dare say two wrongs don't make a right because I know. Yes I have to let wicked and sinful people be but if I could without getting punished by you I would.

Michelle Jean
October 29, 2014

Good God in all you do for me truly remember those who have been good and true to me over the years.

Let their goodness count for something in the end and or in the grand scheme of things. But for those who do to get, acknowledge their goodness not because they do to get. And Good God you know those who have been good to me hence it is those people regardless of creed that I ask you remember. I know the good evil does is not recognized; counts as evil. But if the good was genuine and pure, truly good and clean from the heart then let it count for something.

Even if it is one sin that good can cleanse, let the good these people have done for me wash away that one sin.

Good God I realize I have been unfair in the gratitude department. Hence truly remember my pharmacist that helps me whenever he can. I have to show gratitude to him Good God in all fairness. He has helped me and I should have told you this long ago because my mind have and has been bugging me to do this for a while now.

Truly thank you for helping me. I know you do not base life on unfairness nor do you base life off colour of skin. In all my fairness, I too have been unfair hence I truly ask you to forgive me. Help should not come at a price. Help should be truthful, clean and truly giving. Thank you for reminding me of this.

Michelle Jean
October 29, 2014

Good God despite me saying I was not going to go to my family function, I went. I forced my children to go and I had fun. I had the opportunity to have dinner with my mother's family – my family and I truly enjoyed myself.

I truly thank you for not being angry with me because I went. I needed that.

God wi family quiet een.
Wi one away.

Now if only my sister would stop with the converting business.

Church dutty but yet shi waane people fi guh inna it.

Oh well this is her I guess. Religious to the end.

But truly thank you for letting me go and please do not punish me for lying to you. I said I was not going but went. Truly forgive me.

Michelle Jean
October 27, 2014

Good God my dreams are confusing and no I cannot remember them.

Maybe they're not for me to remember but that's okay.

Been looking at certain things pertaining to livity – homes and I truly thank you for getting these things out of my system.

These homes were extravagant. I didn't even know luxury mansions like these existed in Canada, especially Vaughn, Ontario. Good God I guess this is welcome to the lifestyle of the rich and famous for me. I was wowed and awed by this beauty. Do I want a home like this for me and you?

Yes and no. I need a huge house but this house and or home must be truly inviting and comfy – comfortable. I am not taking away from this house. It is truly beautiful. Maybe I needed this house in BC – British Columbia.

Yes I can live in this house. It's grand from outer to inner. Truly love it hence greed is not in my thought just pure clean and grand livity – beauty. Yes the house and me. Yes I am confused but truly this is the house for me.

Michelle Jean
October 27, 2014

Ah Good God it's so funny how things are changing.

It's October 27, 2014 and Good God black people have become so tattooed and I am asking you in goodness and in truth to overlook certain tattoos. I truly don't like them – tattoos. But because I see them on family members and I truly love my family, please do not charge them for marking their bodies.

I know tattoos are sinful, but Good God my body is marked naturally, so please find it in your heart to forgive us for marking our skin. But Good God full body markings that have tattoos here there and everywhere like in some rappers, singers, basketball players, actors and actress, body sculpture and paint, art; I cannot forgive. They are way too much and they look nasty. You know what Good God forget my asking because tattoos are nasty. Just truly forgive my family members for getting tattoos. They are my true love, some not all. So truly forgive my cousin and nephew for their tattoos.

I know the power of the rose and lion. This power can be felt because I feel it in him. The truth and significance of why he did it I know. For him his tattoo symbolizes truth – true love. Hence I ask you to see the power in the Lyons Lyon and the beauty in us which is your beautiful and delicate rose. You Good God is our beauty hence the lion and the rose, the true you; Jews. Yes tattoos are wrong but truly forgive him because he truly does not know. I truly love you, you know this hence walk and talk with me because our lives are changing. I know the beauty of family Good God and who I truly truly love; you know I truly love. I have to eat with them you know this. I have to share with them like I do with you. So Good God, let true love and truth be yours and mine always and forever. Let us including my family – mother and father's side of the family join as one in unity and truth, true love for more than all eternity but for more than forever ever without end.

Dear God if only you knew just how much I truly love you. Thank you for letting me go to my family's yesterday. We are not dead nor are we dry. We are true and will forever ever be true. We need you. I need you in the midst of us. So truly thank you more than so and more than universal for letting me go.

Michelle Jean
October 27, 2014

P.S. I am truly proud of you. Truly thank you for being more than you to me yesterday.

Good God I truly have to talk to you. It's October 27, 2014 and my brother called me early morn. We were talking about vampires and werewolves. He did more of the talking and I did more of the listening.

Good God, he was associating lesbians and gays to vampires. He said once you are bit you can't go back to being heterosexual.

He says you are punished for being lesbian and gay. He brought up an associate he knew that was gay. Said his daughter fell down and was in a coma. She had a good job in France and he was being punished because he was gay.

He also said the man went to Africa (he's African); moved back to Africa and he consulted a spiritualist and the spiritualist told him the man he was being punished. But my brother associated this punishment for him the man being gay.

Good God you and I know better. The man isn't being punished for being gay. If you are true to yourself and you are clean and true, you cannot be punished. Impossible! You and I know this Good God. No one can be punished by you for the truth. This is infinitely true. But it does not mean that wicked and evil people – humans can't side with all that is evil to cause you pain, punish you. They will, hence humanity is run and governed by wicked and evil people; the clergy as well as wicked and evil men and women in government and the judicial system of the wicked and evil.

See Good God, my brother never thought this man could have killed someone.

He never thought that this man may have used obeah or voodoo to hurt or even kill someone.

He never thought this man could have hurt his mother and father; family.

He never thought about this man's business dealings.

He never thought this man could have been romantically and sexually linked to a person you told him not to be with. Someone you told him not to lie with or get involved with. All these things and more my brother never thought of, hence he associated this man's punishment to homosexuality, lesbian and gayness.

My brother is wise yes but he needs to know the full truth when it comes to the truth of life.

Am I defending homosexuality?

Yes I am Good God because I know men are the dirty and unclean ones.

Was not Satan a man that lied to and deceived Eve?

Is it not man – wicked and evil men that want to dominate and control? And if they don't get their way, they do all to destroy; kill. So evil hath nothing to do with women but have all to do with men. And yes I know not all men are wicked and evil.

They want dominance and control and if they can't have dominance and control they destroy and kill it all. Life is not about control Good God, it's about truth and cleanliness. You cannot live dirty and think for clean people.

You cannot live dirty and then turn around and tell a clean person what to do. You the dirty one is making that clean person dirty.

You cannot say you know but yet live nasty; dirty. Come on now.

Clean should not interact with dirty but we do anyway.

Tell me something. When our clothes are dirty, do we not wash it clean?

So why can't we as human beings wash ourselves clean?

Bathing your skin and washing your clothes isn't clean, meaning fully clean. You have to wash the spirit clean and in order to become fully clean you have to give up sinful and wicked things.

Good God reproducing and having children does not make you clean. It's making you dirty. Many of us including me laid and or lay with dirty men. Some lay with dirty women. So when clean lay with dirty – filth and or filthy, that good person becomes unclean therefore having unclean and or sinful and wicked children.

Remember Good God that your children are all females and we are forbidden by law and you to lay with anyone unclean. Clean can only lay with clean hence your children laid with each other. Meaning, laid with clean people and not dirty people. So homosexuality is not dirty, it is clean. Modern day society makes homosexuality unclean. A true homosexual have no desire to reproduce because it is through reproduction that sinful and wicked children comes.

Evil is always trying to reproduce with clean; good and clean people. This is a must for evil. Hence Satan lied to Eve and reproduced with her, therefore causing the children of Eve to become evil, dirty and unclean. And because of this, Earth is unbalanced, meaning there is more sin than there is good. And yes this is why the poles of earth are shifting today. Negative energy must dominate and control but this will come to an end shortly.

Evil is deceiving hence the Book of Sin was written in layers – the layers of death especially Genesis which is the beginning of wickedness; all that is sinful and evil; wicked. But this is in fact not true. Genesis is dealing with the genes of man, hence genetics – the genetic manipulation of man. Therefore Genesis stand for the genes is.

Good God, when did the truth of goodness become evil; the lies of men?

Remember it is a man that brings his filth to a woman in the form of lies and diseases; deceit. You know this, so how can man say they know and have the truth when they are evil?

Goodness starts with a woman, you because you are female in the living – physical and male in the spiritual. You are clean and you like and truly love all who are clean.

So homosexuality for us females and some males are not dirty it is clean. You must stay clean and true to you. Once you leave the realm of clean and go into the realm of unclean; truly good luck because all hell is open unto you. This is what has happened to Blacks and the different races in the time of old and it is still happening today.

Reproduction is a sin when nastiness is involved. So those who do not want to reproduce – have babies are highly blessed and favoured. They do not contribute to the house and whore houses of sin. They shut sin down hence sins people (heterosexuals) do not like them. Sin cannot come to life through them. Impossible if they are true to self and Good God.

If we as heterosexuals and lesbians want and need kids we are to pray to you Good God and Allelujah in goodness and in truth and ask you, bug you for good, true, honest, clean, righteous and positive children void of all sin and evil not just in the physical but in the spiritual as well. This is how we are to pray before we have children. This is the law but none in humanity do this before we have children including me.

Hence because I know, I pray this way for my children and future grand kids and generations infinitely and indefinitely without end forever ever in this day and time.

Yes my children give me trouble but I still pray good for them at times. I still tell Good God I want and need to leave them.

Why?

They need to know the value of Good Life – Truth.

Michelle Jean

Good God as humans we cannot take up the lies of religion and think all is going to be okay because it's not.

We cannot say this is wrong when we know for ourselves it is right.

Separation is a right because as humans, physical and spiritual beings, we are to separate from all evil. We are to do that which is right. We are not to do that which is wrong.

Dear God to interrupt my thought. But Good God what is it between me and death?

Now I remember one of my dreams. Dreamt I was at a dead house – funeral home. The funeral home was huge. I don't know if I sat down to rest my head – fall asleep, but all I remember was these three monkeys. I call them monkeys but they were not like your typical monkeys. They were small and had a round tails on their rear. The tail is not like a peacock feather but peacock feather is nice and round and or oval and the monkey's tail were like this. I don't know if they were excited to see me but they were excited. They were jumping as if jumping on me but I would not let them. I tried to get away from them but I am not sure if one jumped on me and bit me on the finger. All in all though, I left but did not escape these monkeys because

I was still on the funeral home grounds. Walking I saw these people in business attire. 2 White men but I am not sure if the woman, lone white woman was Babylonian. So I held on to one of the white man's hand. I think he was in a Brown if not grey suit but not too sure. So I held his hand and he led me back to the front of the funeral home. But while he was leading me back to the funeral home I tried not to step in feces and the big worms. But did I escape the monkeys? No. So Good God please secure me from death. I know it's coming down to the end of 2014 and this is the time when death go all out to kill me. For some strange reason, I am more vulnerable coming down to the end of the year. Death must pull out all the stops and they are doing so right now. So please truly secure me and my family for another year. And if it be thy will, let death and all that is sinful and evil that is trying to kill me fall before me right away.

Good God truly protect me forever ever and not let death take me. The truth has to be known so return all that is wicked and evil back to sender and truly secure me and all my family from the blows and set ups of death; wicked and evil people including spirits.

Good God this truly has to stop. Death can no longer take us at will and if it is something my children are doing to let death find me, please truly talk to my children and tell them what they are doing is wrong.

It it's me, find a way to show me my wrongs so that I can correct them in goodness and in truth.

Good God, why should I be the continuous target for death?

Do you not think I am tired?

I don't even know what these three monkeys mean.

I don't even know where death is coming from.

Do the three monkeys represent three deaths in my family?

Or does it represent marriage?

Good God I don't know anymore because death is all around me.

These three monkeys would not leave me alone. Hence I have to wonder if they are the three daughters of Eve.

Ah Good God I am confused.

You know what Good God; I have to find a way to vacation soon. I know there is no escaping death but I have to escape you. You are not true to me because you keep leaving the door open for death to find me and this is so not fair. Nor is it just and right to me. I see so much death and I am truly tired.

Why is death showing me this? I know, I am the intended target of death but Good God why can't you truly shut death down infinitely and indefinitely when it comes to me?

Michelle Jean
October 27, 2014

Good God and Allelujah, do you want death to kill me?

Do you want death to take me to hell with him and her?

So if the answer is no. Why is it coming down to the end of the year, death is pulling out all the stops with me?

It's bad enough my health is crap and you refuse to direct me to the right medicines that can help me.

It's bad enough that I've been complaining to you for years about my health issues and you've turned the other cheek; a blind eye. I am tired of this. Like I've said, you want us to listen to you but you refuse to listen to me; us.

See just how unfair you are to me Good God. I choose life, but yet death still affects me. I am not life and death. I am true life because I truly love life; you. Neither one of us should be both; we should be the truth, hence void of all sin and death; evil.

I don't know Good God but why do you keep letting me down?

Why the hell do you keep failing me?

Why the hell do you anger me?

I am tired of reminding you of truth and true love. You know what, truly go and leave me the hell alone because you are no use to me. You are a failure not just in the physical but in the spiritual. Hence I am jumping ship because I find no truth in you anymore. And hell no, death bleep the hell off because I more than infinitely and indefinitely truly do not choose you or want you in my life. I don't need you either so truly leave me the hell alone.

My God – THE TRUE AND LIVING GOD HAVE TO FIND HIMSELF WHEN IT COMES TO ME BEFORE HE CAN TALK TO ME AGAIN.

Michelle Jean

Good God are you old and senile? No don't answer that. You are as tired as me and need your body to recharge.

Ah Good God I have to leave you alone. I truly don't want to be here but here I am.

Need to cut my hair real soon.

Need to truly do me.

Yes after the winter I'll cut my hair. It's growing but that's it for me.

These three monkeys are getting me to think.

Maybe it's see no evil.
Hear no evil.
Speak no evil.

But Good God, how can I not see hear and speak when all around me is littered with filth and evil?

Maybe the international community is going to try and shut me up and down. But Good God are you truly going to let wicked and evil people shut me and you down? Even try to kill me. Good God the death of me is also the death of you – all life on a whole.

You are God – Good God and the truth needs to be known. Do not let evil kill the truth because truth is what we as humans need. ***Truth is everlasting life.*** Many of us have truth. So truly do right and just by us. You cannot let wicked and evil people including corporations shut us down. You cannot continue to let this happen. You need to be fair and just and you also need to know where your priorities lie. Remember you are the one to choose us, so when we are doing true, right and just by you and all, you have to keep the truth going. You cannot under any circumstances let death take away your truth, our truth from all. Come on now. Truly do better because none of us that you've chosen signed up to die for anyone or anything including the wicked and evil.

Michelle Jean
October 27, 2014

Like I said Good God, you are not fair. Evil rise up and kill.

If evil and wicked people do not like the truth, they do all to kill you. They do all, but I am not running. I will continue to speak the truth despite the way death tries to kill me and set me up.

You show me this before it happens yes and I truly thank you for this. But it's time wicked and evil people be shut down infinitely and indefinitely forever ever without end.

I cannot shut down evil alone. Earth has to help by withholding her goodness and truth to wicked and evil people in wicked and evil lands.

You have to help also Good God because in all of this, Good Truth and Goodness; Positivity and Cleanliness must be in the midst of all we do and that's you.

Evil must be stopped Good God. Evil must be stopped.

Dear God, evil kills good all the time but yet you continue to see this and let it happen.

Tell me are good people slaves to the wicked? I am trying and I need you to defend me and stand firm with me all around.

I need you hence I am leaning on you and eating with you in goodness and in truth. Good God, the separation of Good and Evil must begin again and you must be truly with us in the midst of all that we do that is good and true. We can no longer let wicked and evil people kill us; it defeats the purpose of life. You are merciful Good God. Please truly have good and true mercy for your children including Earth. Earth must also stand firm and true to your people because she too is involved in this. She too is a part of Good and True Life and I refuse to exclude her.

Michelle Jean
October 27, 2014

Good God you know that man – men in the physical realm is Satan. And no one can dispute this because this was recorded in the Book of Sin. Man's or Sins nasty beginning. Genesis as recorded by man is the first book hence the nastiness and lies are recorded in sins beginning. But Good God you and I know that true life is born and sin and or death is born also. Hopefully I will get to explain this to man in another book on a different level.

Good God the creation of man has different stages – hence man's false beginning.

Until this day man has been lying to women and it has to stop Good God. Come on now. I know most of the truth. You had to separate from man – humanity. You are both male and female Good God, male in the spiritual realm and female in the living – physical. Humanity knows not this so every chance I get I remind them in these books.

You are with us. You cannot forget us because we reside in the physical you; earth and this is why man tries so hard in the living (physical) to destroy women.

For them they have to dominate and control us but you cannot continue to let this happen Good God come on now. Life is about truth and goodness hence goodness must prevail at all times. You cannot let goodness die with sin. It is simply not fair come on now.

The hatred have to stop Good God hence the spiritual good must unite with the physical good.

Good God you have to unite in goodness with Mother Earth. You cannot let the evils and wickedness of man continue to destroy her; you. Satan set out to prove a point and humans – humanity gave Satan the victory over you. Humanity bargained away their lives and aligned with death against you and now death comes to take them home.

Yes these are the final years, seconds of man and if we don't change self now we are all doomed.

144 000 000 say man hence only 144 000 000 not 144 000 must be saved. 144 000 000 hath life but death has billions because man did give their lives over to death and you have to make it so Good God.

You cannot change the will of man Good God. Hence man – humanity will learn the hard way never to trust the devil because evil cannot change nor will evil stop deceiving people –

humanity. Good God you know this so truly let the evils of man – humanity stop – be done.

Death is whom billions selected over you so truly give humanity what they want without regret. Like I've told you, if someone do not want you and or did not choose you leave them alone.

You cannot fight for people that truly do not care about you or truly love you. You are fighting in vain as well as fighting a losing battle. You know this because after all is said and done, that person is still going to yearn and crave the god that you saved them from. They will eventually leave you, hence you deceived yourself into thinking that that person was true. Sometimes I feel this way with you. I feel as if I am deceiving myself with you and this is truly not fair. You cannot say do but yet the person is doing and you make them feel like a failure in all they do when it comes to you.

You cannot be fair to the unjust whilst leaving those that truly love you unfed.

Death's children do not care about you, so truly care for your true own. Show them you truly love them and save them from that which is to come. Yes it's great that you remember us, you've not forgotten us. But remembering us in my book cannot save us the way I need you to save us.

Yes I know I am truly wrong in saying this but I truly need you to think because in many ways I am confused and leery of you.

I know I know I am truly wrong. But when I see all that is happening, I have to get leery of you. Evil is still winning and this is truly wrong. I need true and clean, good and pure justice and I hate waiting for this. I know you cannot speed up time and change time but you can do something to help us now for the greater good; better.

And no I do not want or need to let you go forever ever, but I have to come to you with my reservations when I have reservations. You are my true hope for a better tomorrow and I cannot give you up. And stepping aside as of 2015 January 1 is not letting you go. I cannot let you go Good God because you are truly rooted in my DNA. I just need a better and clean today and tomorrow. I know it's unfair to put all on you but I have to because this is you and me.

This is why I talk about true love so much. Why do we want to hurt you so Good God?

Why do we want to give up sure for unsure? Yes I know things are hard with you but is it truly? Is it not our needs and wants, no not needs and wants; greed, yes greed that make us fail in life?

We are not satisfied with what we have hence we yearn and deceive self.

We deceive ourselves into thinking perfection is this and that way when all along perfection is within us all. I truly don't want to change me to please anyone because I am truly perfect with me and by me. You are my concern and yes sometimes headache, but one day full truth and happiness comes. I just want time to speed up and let it happen now. And yes if there was a speed up button to time, I would use it without regret just to know and see all sin and evil on earth and in the spiritual realm including where all evil and sin reside go, go back to their realm and realms infinitely and indefinitely.

Good God I know life cannot interfere with death hence I tell you to let death go with his and her people because death's people are not life's people. Come on now. Why should we have to share your goodness with them? They do nothing but destroy, so why should we clean up their messes for them? We are not the scapegoat for the children of death. Hence I truly want none of death's children and people in our good and true world.

I know Good God that you are not pleased with me for writing these words but if these people don't want you, why should we share you with them? Remember, "OUT OF MANY ONE PEOPLE." Hence you only have 1 deggy deggy people and that one deggy deggy people are the Jews – all those who fall under your good and true, clean and positive flag and banner, that which is the Jamaican Flag – The Flag of Physical Life and the Scottish Flag – The Spiritual Flag of Life hence the White and Blue Nile.

Michelle Jean
October 30, 2014

I know humanity will not put things together Good God hence I need your help to explain this if humanity cannot comprehend.

Life begins at home and if we have not made you our good home then we cannot have life. We will be dead to you.

We will become as the dead and this is what's happened to billions on earth in this day and time and this is sad.

Good God you are true to me even though I cast doubt on you. Made you my doubting stick and I am truly sorry but I do not have another avenue. And to be honest I truly don't need another avenue because I've made you my all.

Good God you are not judgmental and you are there because you remember us in time all will be well. But like I said, I want time to speed up and this is wrong.

Good God I need to be with you right now someplace clean. So can you truly blame me for wanting evil and wicked people to be gone? The wages of sin is death and I know we have all sinned. But why can't we show you our true love of you?

I mean we say we love you but yet do all to hurt you. You've tried so hard with us and for us, but yet we've done nothing to truly help you. Instead, we willingly hand ourselves over to death and when it's too late we come a running to you for hope and help.

Look at how you've tried throughout the ages and what have we done? We continuously reject you and accept death. So how fair are we to you?

How can we say we love you but yet turn around and hurt you so?

Michelle Jean
October 30, 2014

It's October 30, 2014 Good God and I feel like I am the crazy one.

Good God no one caught on to this?

Is it just me or did the world miss something here?

Tell me something, are we awake or are we truly dead to what's happening in the world today?

I just saw the RISE OF THE PLANET APES AND I AM BLOWN AWAY BY THIS MOVIE. No one caught the truth hence I ask, am I the only one?

AM I THE CRAZY ONE?

The Rise of the Planet Apes was about Ebola and the transmission of this virus to humans. The virus was created in a lab using apes. This virus was then taken to Africa and from Africa the virus would spread globally. The end of the movie showed you the path the virus would take.

Wow. Unbelievable, hence I am the crazy one. And not there are no conspiracy theories here, just the facts; truth.

Now tell me this Good God, when does it end?

Why do you constantly sit aside and watch the evils of man and do nothing?

Yes I am aware of the time line of death and the choice we've made. But who decides who lives and who dies?

Yes I know about sin and the cost of our sins, but when does it truly stop; end?

Who the hell gives another human being the right to decide who lives and who dies? Yes this is a selective process by others and this is wrong. Why the hell should one play the grim reaper by massacring an entire nation – continent and her people?

Who the bleep are they Good God? Yes I am yelling at you and I am truly angry because no one has the right to do this. How the hell can you say you remember us and permit someone to kill hundreds of millions of people? No come on now. Yes death needs to deal with his and her own and this should not concern me, but it does. I have to get involved because death is only concerned with the sin and sins of man. This is the only way death can take a life. **_The law specifically states, "THE WAGES OF SIN IS DEATH." Man cannot step in and play the_** *__role of death for death. Death has the name and number of all who are to go to hell and die. And for someone in the flesh to expedite the process by massacring hundreds of millions of people in the living is infinitely and indefinitely wrong.__ So because of this Good God Allelujah and the breaking of the law by these people, death's people overstepping their boundaries; you can override death and say, Death, because of what your children has and have done, all in humanity is spared; saved. I know you can do this but I will not beg you for this because I've made up my mind on certain things in life. So because of this, I will leave things alone and I will not spare all because earth have to be rid of all wicked and evil people including spirits. And I've told you, I will not save anyone that is wicked and evil if I am the saving grace for humanity. But if there was a way to do this, stay death without saving wicked and evil people including wicked and evil spirits I would, but I can't.*

__Onwards I Go__

But why Africa Good God?

Why Africa?

You said you remember us, well do something. Truly remember us and do something to save Africa and Africa's people because what death's people are doing is wrong.

The Herod's of the world is wrong and you have no right to see this and do nothing. You too are wrong. One cannot decide the faith and or life of another. <u>You don't draw lots when it comes to life because all life is important and life was given not stolen.</u>

I was asked to make a decision in the Instructions For Death. I did what I needed to do and I stand by that decision.

But no one has the right to choose who lives and who dies. None one signed up for this hence I tell humanity to know you and know how you speak – tell them things; the truth.

Who the hell are these people Good God? Hence the virus (new strain of virus) is going to spread further than Africa because it will become airborne. The drug that WHO is developing isn't to save Africans, but to further kill them and others in humanity. Hence European Nations and China won't know what hit them. Bye bye Russia, France, Spain, Italy, Scotland and Iceland. Good bye my Caribbean Islands and Southern Lands.

Hence a global pandemic worse than the black plague will destroy billions if something isn't truly done to stop this virus collectively globally. THE WAR ON MAN – HUMANITY HAS BEGUN, HENCE THE KILLING FIELDS OF MODERN DAY HUMANS – MAN. Killing machines will no longer kill man. Man has found a more invasive and deadlier way to kill. Man has and have designed and created medicines and manmade infectious diseases. Diseases that halter our physical structure on a molecular level, diseases designed to kill – wipe out nations at will.

This is the beginning of the black race because this is the last of days and all black people must die; go to hell and burn like him Satan.

Babylon won Good God, hence truly woe be unto man because a new plague has been unleashed and humanity will have hell to pay literally.

Dear God, why did they do this?

Like I said, you did not lock anyone out of your abode. We did this all on our own. Now truly look at the cost to life and our lives on earth and in the spiritual realm.

Who the hell are these people to play Gods?

You of yourself do not decide who lives and who dies. You cannot because life has nothing to do with death, but yet these people kill; select who lives and who dies. Good God this is wrong. You gave no one this right not even me. And no, the Instructions For Death does not give me the right to choose in my book.

Am I truly angry at you?

Yes because in all you did, you did not prepare your people properly. Hence the selection has begun and it is the black race as always must be the first to go; die.

You permit this always hence I ask you, what gives you or anyone the right to choose who lives and who dies?

Yes you choose to me Good God because you see this happening but yet do nothing about it. Now tell me this, with all this said, who is going to stand up with me and charge THE UNITED STATES OF AMERICA FOR GENOCIDE AND CRIMES AGAINST

HUMANITY – LIFE? Hence I declare judgment on you Good God and Allelujah. I declare judgment on you because you see the wrongs of Babylon, the United States of America and do nothing to stop them. They are not gods but yet each and every day they play god – the god of death. No one chose them to speak for life, but yet they overstep their authority and speak anyway. America cannot speak for life because they have not life. Hence they are the Valley of Death; all that is dead; evil.

How can you be okay with this Good God? This land is the valley of death and people are dying globally because of them. Hence when death talks about sin America and its people is whom death talk about. You know this and I know this. But in all that I've said, you readily condemn my homeland but not them. Well I condemn them due to the evils and wrongs they have done. You cannot play favorites. Both lands are wrong so why condemn one and not the other?

Look at Sudan and the pitting against North and South by an American.

Look at the diseases that these people have unleashed on African lands and people including others and you've done nothing to wake these people up and warn them.

"THOU SHALT NOT KILL," BUT BABYLON – THE UNITED STATES OF AMERICA KILL ANYWAY. Now tell me, are they an exception to the rule; your laws?

You let them willingly kill; hence I am angry and yelling at you once again.

Good God a nation of people should not have to die because Herod and his people do not like them.

Dear God, truly have mercy on Africa and her people because all that the devil's people are doing is wrong. I am asking you to truly remember Africa and her people.

*Dear God if mi affi roll a dutty fi yu fi hear me when it comes to Africa I will. Good God no, this isn't right man this isn't right. One nation cannot be the scapegoat and sacrificial lambs for sins children and people globally. The killing has to stop hence I declare Judgment on the United States of America for the evils that they have done to humanity globally. **The eradication of***

hundreds of millions even billions is not for the one to decide. The one have no say in our lives. Each and every individual has his or her own right and rights and they must live by them according to the law and laws of Life.

Every evil and sinful wall that they knowing and willingly set up must come tumbling down. Every sin that they have done must return unto them and land. Thus saith the Lord thy God because she is angry and angry at you Good God and Allelujah. You are truly not fair. The wages of sin is death and these people have and has gone beyond protocol. Hence I declare judgment on you and the United States of America. You cannot be wicked to your people, this is wrong. I know you are hurt but the pain must stop because like I said, we are a nation of people that truly do not listen. You have to set death's people straight Good God, hence I must set death straight. Death must abide by the laws of death. Because America, the United States of America goes against the protocol of death you death have to look into this. You have the mandate of what is going to happen hence I declare judgment on Good God and Allelujah and the United States of America. The wages of sin is death hence you must go by this law and look into the wrongs of the United States of America from the past right up to today. You cannot allow them to take anymore lives by playing and or masquerading as you. I will not allow this nor am I telling you to kill them. You have all the evidence against them hence I am putting my case forward in the courthouse of life, you Good God and Man including Death. I will not allow them (the United States) to continue preying on others or anyone else Good God. If I am wrong to do this Good God please forgive me because I will not turn the other cheek when it comes to injustice of another human and or human beings. Death has all the ammunition against the United States hence you must step aside and let these people go.

You cannot condone the wrongs of them. I will not let you hence I will cast judgment on you. I am not going against you; I am just doing what you cannot do for the better good of humanity and Mother Earth.

You have to let wicked and evil people go.

They have sinned vile and wicked and you let them continue to do this. Hence where is your power to do that which is right and just by humanity; clean?

How can you say you need me but yet you are unjust?

Humans are not allowed to take human life and you and death know this, but yet shut your mouths whilst making humans take each other's lives.

The law is clear but yet both sides are willing to break them. So where is the fairness in life if we break the law and laws of life?

Are we not sinful?

All the evidence is there for death. Every stone, every jot of blood that America – the United States of America or anyone spills is there on record. These sins are punishable by law – the laws of Good and Evil – Life. But yet you Good God and Allelujah protect America – the United States of America from this. They rejected Marcus Mosiah Garvey hence rejecting you.

California has and have banned the Southern Cross our Confederate Flag of THE SOUTH for being displayed every day. *Yes the flag is not banned for special functions but a ban is a ban. There is no banning half way because there are no half truths just lies. Now the question I ask is, why when I was shown the Washington Monument Falling in one of my dreams?*

Why do you allow them to continuously kill?

Are you not guilty of sin if allow this to continuously happen?

Yes we sold you out hence the Babylonian Jews lie to humanity about Satan. They did take the offer of sin hence they did write Sins book for Him. Told humanity Satan Tempted Jesus and offered him all, but what they did not tell us was that they the Babylonian Jews did accept the offer of sin hence the Holy Book (Bible) of modern day man – men.

Good God our sins determine where we go, hence it is death that is to take us. Yes I know death can be in human form and this is wrong. We as humans do the taking for death – Black Death and we are wrong to do this. **When you (a person or anyone) make sacrifices onto death, you are locking yourself as well as your family out of the good and true abode of Good God. <u>Once you are locked out of Good God's kingdom and or abode, you are infinitely and indefinitely locked out. You cannot get back in and this is what happened to Adam and Eve of your book of sin. Hence you were told a flaming sword was placed in the gateway of Eden so that Adam and Eve could not get back in.</u>** *No one can change this if they are not ordained to do so. Once you're locked out you are locked out. Hence Good God cannot save people that are not his.*

The selective process is also wrong. And yes I am sorry I had to declare judgment on you Good God but I had to. Yes I was angry but you need to truly listen and see. I truly love you but I cannot stand aside and look. If we as black people continue to be stubborn and not learn, then yes walk away forever ever from us indefinitely. You cannot keep trying with stiff necked and stubborn people that don't listen. You send your messengers and no one can tell you whom to choose to deliver your message. Humanity has to learn that you cannot send someone that is not of you – your flag and life to represent you. So after this harvest, truly do not extend your lifeline to man and or humanity again. Save your people and teach them true and right in all that you do. But let Death take his and her people indefinitely to his realm; home. You cannot save Death's children and people because they are not yours. You have to let them go with death to never ever return to earth. Earth belongs to you and your good people hence goodness must reign supreme forever ever without end indefinitely in a good and positive way.

Do not stand aside anymore and look; but take all your goodness from wicked and evil people including lands. We can no longer disrespect you and think what we are doing is right because it is wrong. ***Good God we have been deceived. Look how many globally that has***

made sacrifices to death for riches and a position in hell. All these people who have made sacrifices think they are going to go to heaven because Satan is their king and god so they do all for him. But pity they do not know that Satan did not create anything and Satan cannot give them a home on earth no matter how much they make sacrifices unto him. The more they kill is the more death takes and you and I know this. Their home is hell hence many are going to ball more than a bitch in heat in hell.

Good God you deserve better and every one deserve a chance to choose you.

No one has the right to choose for us but us.

No one has the right to play death because death has a job to do and he and she alone must do it. Thus saith the Lord thy God meaning it is so. So truly forgive me Good God and Allelujah for overstepping my boundaries with you but I had to in my anger.

We all have a choice Good God and it is not right for anyone to take this right from us. Humans were not to kill but yet we kill anyway. You are Good God and Allelujah and you cannot let the guilty go free. You

have an obligation to all life whether good or bad.

You have all the evidence, let justice be truly done. Billions of people are on this planet Good God. It is our sins – choice to sin that kills us. Someone should not decide for us because they have no right to do so. Not even death can choose who lives and who dies. Come on now. ***It is not up to a human how we die, it is up to death how he or she takes you due to your sins. Hence it is our sins that determine when and how we die.***

Both life and death have a choice and we've been making that choice. No one has the right to play Herod and or continue with the Herod massacre come on now. Fair is fair Good God hence you truly do not need me. You would rather hundreds of millions of people go to their graves because someone selected them to die rather than do things the right way.

No I am not defending the process of death. I am just defending the right to life and death for both Good and Evil. Like I said, our sins are what kills us and no one should expedite the death process not even me. Yes I want death's people to be gone indefinitely but there is a process that must be followed and or be adhered to.

If your name and number is on death's true docket, then let death come and do his and her job. No one should have to do their job for them.

Killing someone because someone says so is wrong. Humanity can no longer be the sacrifices for sin – Satan come on now.

He lied whilst deceiving Adam and Eve and it has to stop.

Someone cannot tell us to sin reckless because someone is going to save us. This is never going to happen because we were told, "THE WAGES OF SIN IS DEATH." So if we sin, how can anyone override this? No one can override death if your name and number is on the docket of death. Hence your SIN – SOCIAL INSURANCE AND OR SOCIAL

SECURITY NUMBER. See how long that number is? Now you have an idea of how long your time in hell will be.

Michelle Jean

It's November 1, 2014 early morning and I truly have to ask you Good God about fairness. I have to ask you about morals and ethics.

Where is man's morals and ethics when it comes to life?

Where do you stand in all of this?

Dear God have we come this far that we have to eliminate others under the quiet?

Are they so smart at what they do that you as God – Good God and Allelujah can't stop these people?

Now I ask you this good God, why us?

Why let us die like this?

Have we been so conditioned to believe in all that is superficial when it comes to you?

Now I ask, do you truly exist for the better good of man – humanity and the earth?

We believe so much in you that you have failed us. So at what point do we (your people) stop believing in you?

At what point do we say bleep you, you do not exist and you are not a part of Life's Good Source?

Good God no one can sit on the sidelines and watch death – humans take it all.

Hundreds of millions will die Good God because of manmade diseases; hundreds of millions that did not get a fighting chance because someone selected death for them. Someone took their lives from them. So at what point do you as God step in and say this isn't right nor is it the way. Like I said, ***the right to die is not up to a human, it is up to death due to our sins.*** When we sin we die. It is not for humans to take another's life, it is up to death and death only if we sin. Yes death can take you by any means necessary but it is wrong for death to use humans in the by any means necessary method. In truth humanity knows not the truth when it comes to life and death nor do we care to know the truth. ***We were told "TRUTH IS EVERLASTING LIFE" but yet we sin and tell lies anyway.*** If we know that truth is life, why live to die?

In all I've blasted you Good God and cast doubt upon you. But do you blame me from what I see and know?

Maybe I am crazy but like I said, who gives another human being the right to choose who lives and who dies?

Who gives them the right to cast lots like I've said? You do not cast lots on anyone, so why should anyone cast lots when it comes another?

To interrupt the editing of this book Good God, it's November 02, 2014 and yesterday I read on Bossip where this teacher said if she had 15 minutes to live she would kill all black people. Good God I forgive her, truly forgive her because the black race has been on the extinction list of everyone for centuries. It matters not to me anymore who wants to kill every black person globally because as black people we have no ambition for self and I refuse to fight for people who care not for the truth – their own lives.

I cannot deal with the hate of our own and if our own continually accept this hate, then who am I to want better for them; our own. Should my own not want better for self?

As for you the teacher in the United States of America that want this for all blacks like I said, I forgive you but I will never forget this because you are the second person to say this. ***Remember what goes around comes around. I do not want death for white people or any race for that matter. Everyone has a right to life and like I said, we as humans give up our lives to death. And like I said, I do not care how death takes his and her people because the children and people of death is not my concern. Truth, the children and people of Good God and Allelujah is my concern. By you saying you would kill all black people if you had fifteen minutes to live you've condemned every American globally. You've condemned Puerto Rico, Guam, American Samoa, US Virgin Islands, Hawaii, The United States of America and their Allies INFINITELY AND INDEFINITELY WITHOUT END***

FOREVER EVER. YOUR LANDS CANNOT BE SAVED IN THIS HARVEST AND NOTHING THAT ANYONE DO OR DOES WILL SAVE THEM. THEY ARE CONDEMNED INDEFINITELY. None can or will rise again after the harvest comes and is done. Allelujah, let thy good will be done Good God and Allelujah. So said so done and so condemned. Thus saith the Lord thy God meaning it is so.

ONWARDS I GO because I will not change this condemnation. Hence Good God truly take your people out of wicked and evil lands. If they (your true people) refuse to leave let them be. Let them go down like Job's wife who turned a pillar of salt according to their book of sin; the dead. Yes their so called holy bible.

Humans are not experiments but yet to the few that control humanity we are. You want all for self but yet all was not given unto you.

As humans we've given law makers, politicians; religious clergies – men and woman, doctors, death, our parents, pharmaceutical companies including you Good God and Allelujah the right to have a say in our lives. We trust all to do right and good by us, but no one has our best interest at heart. None can do right and just by us and this is a crying shame. We say we love but yet hate our fellow man.

No one is willing to be truthful to us and our lives. So they do all to keep you in the dark, do all they can to deceive and kill. But in all that we do as humans, we forget the consequences of sin – our sins.

Why lead if you are false?

Why lead if you have no good will for the people you serve and or claim to love. Life has come down to profit money Good God and this is wrong.

Listen to One Drop by Bob Marley Good God. We need your true teachings not the devil's philosophy.

Like I said, you permit things to happen hence I question you.

You are suppose to be the greatest authority figure, but you have no authority over man. Just like the

diseases of man you cannot control man.

You cannot do right by us.

Yes I know the laws of sin but man – humanity has gone beyond the protocol of death. Man has and have created their own sinful societies without you.

Man dominates and you are just a figment of our imagination because in truth, the societies of man (evil societies) do not include you nor do they believe in you.

You've been excluded long ago, hence they've (evil) created their own wicked and evil; sinful societies based on greed; financial gain, domination and control and there's not a damned thing you can do about it.

Evil locked you out of your own creation. So truly what say you?

Yes we have the billionaires but they do not run the world. He does. Hence his pocket book isn't

<u>in billions but in trillions. Add up all the gold, oil reserves, the global financial market and he runs it all; have it all because the wealth accumulated by the different societies of sin – Satanic Societies truly belong to him and not them; his children and people. He's the true dark knight of pure and utter evil. No one can stop him because he defeated you by taking you out of the equation. He's given you all that is filthy and dirty hence he runs earth and not you.</u>

In all he did, he sacrificed his children and people unto death hence his children and people do his bidding. They think they are going to go to heaven when he knows they are going to go to hell. They think when they kill all the Jews they will have earth as their domain forever ever indefinitely. But in truth, they will not have earth forever ever indefinitely because Earth – Mother Earth must withhold her goodness from them due to their sins and sinful ways. Earth can do this because as the earth gives life she too can withhold from life – wicked and evil people; wicked and evil life. No one can kill the Jews because none knoweth the truth of the Jews. None knoweth the life of a true Jew. Hence a Jew knows the spirit – Life of All including death. Jews cannot die, because it was the Jews that created it all, hence "OUT OF MANY ONE PEOPLE." Hence only one hath life and not the many in this world.

Good God will always remember the Jews because they are his people and we are his children.

ONWARDS I GO

You're not even a figure Good God because he's made earth so filthy and dirty that you the original creator of all cannot come into the planet you created. So yes he took it all from you and he used your own creation to do it.

He locked you out Good God; hence his people think he is all powerful – untouchable because he has it all including your own children and people.

Yes we can talk and say even rejoice but I know otherwise Good God. I truly know otherwise hence I know the cleanliness of the spirit. The spirit is the governor of our lives and it is because of this governance your people do not have to connect to you with the flesh. We must connect with you and to you via the spirit because the spirit is true life.

Humans cannot kill the spirit but they can kill and take the flesh.

So in all his power and glory Good God, in truth he's not more powerful than you because of time.

Evil hath time hence the time of evil has expired and all that is wicked and evil must shortly pay; come to an end. Yes the harvest comes hence truly woe be unto him and man.

See Good God what man and humanity do not know is that, DEATH WAS GIVEN TIME, HENCE DEATH IS IN TIME; the time to take all that is wicked and evil – sinful. Thus man forgot about time and equated 666 to him Satan instead of remembering that when we kill, death rise up in time to take all who are wicked and evil on a global scale. We all know about Noah and how all died in his time hence man – humanity could not put two and two together in this day and time until now.

In all that we have done, we've forgotten that Good God is a part of our DNA and no one can alter this DNA. Hence the spirit of man you cannot see nor can you find. ***HENCE BOB MARLEY TOLD US IN TIME WILL TELL AND NO ONE LISTENED TO HIM.*** Hence I tell you (my readers) to know how Good God speak to us.

Yes the spirit can be found, but if you know not where to look and what you are looking for, how can you find it? You will never find it.

Michelle Jean
November 1 & 2, 2014

I do not claim to be nor will I claim to be Good God. The evils of man has and have reached higher heights; but yet nothing is done to stop evil.

Evil has expanded completely hence billions bask in their own sins – evils; wealth.

Death comes to take on a massive scale now and this is all due to the sins man; sins that have been adding up for centuries – thousands of years.

With sin there are no ethics or morals just sin; the sins that we do to keep hell going.

Man – humanity hath no morals hence we lie and deceive self each and every day.

You are real Good God hence your life and truth is beyond measure. Yes I have to be this way with you but truly, who has that absolute authority to decide who lives and who dies. Not even death has this power and authority.

I know the power of you but why should one race be the target of all that is sinful and wicked? It's like the fox and the hound and the black race have become the target for all that is sinful and wicked; death.

Yes Black Death sees these things but yet have no say; conscience to say hey you cannot do this. You cannot take a life, this is my job based on the persons sins – wicked and evil deeds.

Black Death have not stepped in to say, wait a minute you cannot speak for me. You are taking my right and rights from me. Who gives you the authority to act on the behalf of me? Well I am exercising my right and let your tree including your ancestral tree, all that is important to you I will take because you've given me the right to do so. Hence your tree will never bare again. As you've taken the trees of life willingly and deceitfully, so shall yours be taken away from you under the laws of Life and Death; Sin.

Man has and have become vile in their day to day lives. Hence under the Laws of Life and Death, all that is wicked and evil must pay because the law specifically say and state, "the wages of sin is death," and death now have to exercise his and her right under the law. Man was never ordained to kill man but yet man – humanity kill any way. Man has and have ordained themselves law givers but yet cannot uphold the law.

Man has and have put themselves above the laws hence they break them each and every day.

Man say they love God but yet hurt and kill him each and every day.

He Good God and Allelujah has and have given us a home on earth but instead of keeping our house; home we destroy it, condemn it with our lies and sins; deceit.

How can a dirty man clean house or even keep it clean?

All that humans were not to do, we have done whilst deceiving self; believing in lies and deceit.

In all we have and has done as humans, we've brought ourselves to the brink of extinction all around.

We failed our god including failed ourselves.

Michelle Jean
November 1and 2, 2014

There is a due process to Life and Death Good God and no one can override this process. No human can because humans cannot create time nor do they know the process of time.

Time is constant and cannot change for anyone or anything.

Time is always there hence all is done in time at that moment in time.

Yes there are different times hence in terms of man – humanity, but in fact there is but one time zone. It is humans that cannot tell true time and we all know this.

Death was given time in time. Hence death was given time to kill – take all that is wicked and evil in time at that moment in time. Hence man and or humanity knoweth not the time and hour for his and her death. Yes the extinction of man on a global scale.

Death isn't for man – humans. Death is for death but in all that humans do, we mess up; sin and think we have a saving grace – going to be okay.

We've forgotten if we are clean we cannot die. Hence death cannot take clean; good and true people. Death can only take unclean – sins children and people.

REMEMBER THIS ALWAYS:

"OUT OF MANY ONE PEOPLE"

Hence we are not all Good God's people and if you are not a JEW, HOW ARE YOU GOING TO BE SAVED?

Michelle Jean
November 1, 2014

Good God as I come to a close with this book I had to get it done before What A Mess. Hopefully I will get What A Mess done shortly. Also forgive me for the many missed words and typos that are in all these books. I do not have an editor and I truly do not know when you are going to send me one. As messengers when you give us a task to do, we cannot involve anyone in that message we have to walk the road alone until you change it. As always do not let the mistakes hinder anyone from learning and truly do not let sin and death use any mistake in these books to get a pass. You are Good God alone and you know what you are doing. Yes I would truly love for these books to be perfect and void of all mistakes but as we make mistakes in life, we will make mistakes in our writings and asking of you. Once again truly forgive me and let all that is good and true for your people be done accordingly in a good and positive, truthful, clean and honest way.

ONWARDS I GO

As God – Good God man you cannot allow and or permit man to draw lots and condemn a nation of people that has done them nothing.

You said you remember us, then do more than remember us but truly help us out of goodness and truth. You are the positive one in all of this. And truly don't look at me because I am hot headed and you know this.

I am not you and in truth I truly don't want or need to be. I truly need to be the good me now. I have truly love me and I need to move on to a better, more positive and beautiful life; me. I can no longer walk in the Valley of Death with you because death is neither you nor is it me.

We need to become fully clean hence I HAVE TO WALK IN THE VALLEY OF LIFE TRUTHFULLY AND CLEAN FOREVER EVER WITHOUT END.

Humans were told man to man is unjust and this is correct because the one have and has cast lots to kill the ONE PEOPLE; your children and people and this is not correct. Hence I ask you, who is going to hold the United States of America guilty for genocide, crimes against humanity and more importantly, crimes against life – you?

As humans we cannot choose death for the next person. This is wrong and you of yourself know this Good God but yet you permit it anyway. Yes I know death hath time to take on a massive scale, but who will speak on the behalf of the innocent?

Who will speak for earth and her trees; waterways and air – environment?

Neither one of us can be unfair to Good God, so why are you acting unfair?

Why do you allow me to think this when it comes to life – the life of your children and people?

In all we as humans have done is take from life. No one, absolutely no one can repay life or create life, but yet we take life from all you've given us without thinking that one day we will pay for our wrongs.

As Good God and Allelujah you are obligated to life and it is with this obligation that I am talking to you now.

You are good life, so why let evil and wicked people continue to take life. Like I've said in other books, I will not interfere with death when it comes to his children. I am not concerned about death's children. I am worried about your people; hence I seek justice for them and me. Only them must I seek justice for because wicked and evil people know the evils that they have done and I refuse to save any of them (wicked and evil people including spirits) if I am the saving grace for the world. You cannot knowingly and willingly sin and expect to be saved, come on now.

We all want to be happy but yet we hurt each other. As long as it's not me I have no concerns and this is fine. Like I've said, if my enemy's house is burning, I will do the godly thing by calling the fire department but I will not run into the fire to save none. You are not clean, you've done all to hurt me and others so why now that hell's fire is consuming you, I should go into hell's fire and save you. I don't want to die like you so I do all to stay out of hell and stay away from hell's children; you. Therefore it is imperative for good to separate from all sin and evil in all that they do.

Life is water not fire, so why would I live to die? No one should, but yet we live to die. We listen to others lie to us without knowing these lies are leading us straight to hell.

Justice has always been the cry of your children Good God and it's time for you to truly listen. We were told to stay out of evil's way.

We are to separate from the wicked and evil; North, but we could not do this hence man have and has tainted your flags of life. So because of this, all flags have and has been returned to you for safe keeping. Humanity is not worthy of them because if they were, they would not sin so much nor would they cause you shame. And no Good God, I am not · worthy because I am hotheaded and I swear.

You as God – Good God and Allelujah should know that you cannot give clean to dirty people. They will dirty what you have given them. Look at how I complain to you about cleanliness. I can't keep up hence many days I give up.

All my children are of age now and it's time I truly find my own. Hence you too Good God must find your own.

You can no longer hold out for hope when it comes to us as humans. We keep deceiving you and this is not right. Let the deceit stop and like I said, once earth has rid itself from all evils and sin, never let sin or evil find a place on earth ever again more than infinitely and indefinitely.

Sin had his and her time. Now it's good's time to save and replenish the earth with all that is good and true, positive and clean.

You cannot give and get dirty in return.
You cannot love us so and get hate in return.

Love is not pure nor is it clean.
True love is the key hence true love is rare.

This is the time of Herod all over again Good God because one race has and have become the sacrificial lambs and this must stop. You cannot allow others to feed us to their gods.

You cannot allow others to take the lives of millions come on now.

"OUT OF MANY ONE PEOPLE." So truly save your one people; your true own.

Like I've said time and time again, life isn't death, it's life and we are to live our lives good, true and clean.

We know truth is everlasting life, so why can't we be true to life all the time?

Murder is murder and you gave no one the right to select one race to die over the next. Come on now.

We need you but you are failing us.

Man should not use the resources of the earth to kill anyone or anything come on now.

Like I said, our sins cause death to come and no one has the right to select anyone to feed to their gods. This is wrong and unethical. Earth is vast and if we as humans had taken care of it (Earth) things would not come to this.

We have a home and instead of keeping it clean we keep it unclean. So if we cannot keep our home clean, how are we going to keep your house clean and tidy Good God?

Michelle Jean

OTHER BOOKS BY MICHELLE JEAN

Blackman Redemption – The Fall of Michelle Jean
Blackman Redemption – After the Fall Apology
Blackman Redemption – World Cry – Christine Lewis
Blackman Redemption
Blackman Redemption – The Rise and Fall of Jamaica
Blackman Redemption – The War of Israel
Blackman Redemption – The Way I Speak to God
Blackman Redemption – A Little Talk With Man
Blackman Redemption – The Den of Thieves
Blackman Redemption – The Death of Jamaica
Blackman Redemption – Happy Mother's Day
Blackman Redemption – The Death of Faith
Blackman Redemption – The War of Religion
Blackman Redemption – The Death of Russia
Blackman Redemption – The Truth
Blackman Redemption – Spiritual War
Blackman Redemption – The Youths
Blackman Redemption – Black Man Where Is Your God?

The New Book of Life
The New Book of Life – A Cry For The Children
The New Book of Life – Judgement
The New Book of Life – Love Bound
The New Book of Life – Me
The New Book of Life – Life

Just One of Those Days
Book Two – Just One of Those Days
Just One of Those Days – Book Three The Way I Feel
Just One of Those Days – Book Four

The Days I Am Weak
Crazy Thoughts – My Book of Sin
Broken
Ode to Mr. Dean Fraser

A Little Little Talk
A Little Little Talk – Book Two

Prayers
My Collective
A Little Talk/A Time For Fun and Play
Simple Poems
Behind The Scars
Songs of Praise And Love

Love Bound
Love Bound – Book Two

Dedication Unto My Kids
More Talk
Saving America From A Woman's Perspective
My Collective the Other Side of Me
My Collective the Dark Side of Me
A Blessed Day
Lose To Win
My Doubtful Days – Book One

My Little Talk With God
My Little Talk With God – Book Two

A Different Mood and World – Thinking

My Nagging Day

My Nagging Day – Book Two
Friday September 13, 2013
My True Love
It Would Be You
My Day

A Little Advice – Talk
1313, 2032, 2132 – The End of Man
Tata

MICHELLE'S BOOK BLOG – BOOKS 1 – 19

My Problem Day
A Better Way
Stay – Adultery and the Weight of Sin – Cleanliness
Message

Let's Talk
Lonely Days – Foundation
A Little Talk With Jamaica – As Long As I Live
Instructions For Death
My Lonely Thoughts
My Lonely Thoughts – Book Two